PUBLISHED BY NICHOLAS THOMPSON

Plant Paradox: Lectin Free Diet Quick & Easy Recipes

to Fight Disease and Control Weight Gain

@ Paul Cook

Published By Nicholas Thompson

@ Paul Cook

Plant Paradox: Lectin Free Diet Quick &

Easy Recipes to Fight Disease and

Control Weight Gain

All Right RESERVED

ISBN 978-87-975002-6-2

TABLE OF CONTENTS

keto Brie And Mortadella Salad: 1

Balsamico Butter And Goat Cheese Salad: 2

Avocado And Halloumi Cheese Salad 4

Feta Cheese And Chicken Salad 6

Coal Slaw 7

Orange And Cranberry Muffins 9

Walnut Bread 12

Cauliflower Breakfast Bake 15

Green Smoothie 18

Avocado Salad And Cilantro-Pesto Chicken 19

Arugula Chicken Salad With Lemon Vinaigrette 21

Chicken Nori Wrap With Cilantro Dip 23

Guacamole Lettuce Boats 26

Roasted Broccoli With Cauliflower "Rice" And Pan-Fried Onions 27

Italian Healthy Breakfast 30

Tasty Breakfast Hash 32

Breakfast Food Scramble 34

Butternut Squash Soup 35

Ginger Carrot Soup 37

Green Pea Soup 38

Super Nutrient Smoothie 40

Fruit, Nut And Seed Oatmeal 41

Green Power Smoothie 42

Citrus Sunrise Juice: 44

Berry Blast Smoothie 45

Tropical Paradise Smoothie 47

Pancake With Coconut Mochi 48

Eggplant Casserole For A Large Gathering 50

Green Bread With Bananas 52

Two Ways Of French Toast 55

Bibimbap 58

Braised Short Ribs (Galbi Jim) 61

Bulgogi 64

Bulgogi Chicken 67

- Apple Pie Smoothie 70
- Spicy Peanut Butter Tempeh & Rice 72
- Vegan Fry-Up 75
- Miso Ramen 79
- Bali Bowl With Tempeh, Peanuts And Tomato Sambal . 82
- Scrambled Tofu Breakfast Burrito 85
- Avocado And Smoked Salmon Wrap: 89
- Sweet Potato And Spinach Frittata: 90
- Coconut Flour Pancakes With Berries 91
- Grilled Chicken Salad With Avocado Dressing 92
- Cauliflower Rice Stir-Fry With Shrimp 93
- Hot Kale Salad 94
- Caesar Salad 96
- Greek Keto Salad 98
- Anchovies And Yellow-Beet Salad 100
- Niquise 101
- Chili Soup 103
- Peach Pancakes 105

Egg And Arugula 108

Sweet Potato And Onion Patties 110

Cabbage-Kale Sauté With Salmon And Avocado 113

Coconut And Almond Flour Muffin 115

Cranberry-Orange Muffin 117

Cinnamon And Flaxseed Muffin 119

Shakshuka 121

Orange-Cranberry Morning Bread 122

Vegan Breakfast Burrito 126

Chickpea And Apple Pesto Pasta 129

Spicy Vegetable Noodle Soup 130

Mixed Vegetable Sichuan 133

Australian Breakfast Omelet 136

Avocado Cups 138

Banana Pancakes 140

Keto Brie and Mortadella Salad:

Ingredients:

- 4 ounces anchovies
- 4 ounces brie cheese
- 1 tbsp green pesto
- 2/3 oz Argula Lettuce.
- 8 oz Mortadella
- 8 cups fresh basil leaves
- ¼ cup mayonnaise
- 7 black olives

Directions:

1. Arrange the olives, thinly sliced moradella, mayonnaise, anchovies, brie cheese and pesto on a plate. Then serve with fresh basil leaves and argula.

Balsamico Butter and Goat Cheese Salad:

Ingredients:

- 8 oz goat cheese
- B tbsp vinegar vinegar
- 1 ounce butter
- 2 oz Baby Spinach
- 1/6 Pumpkin Seeds

Directions:

1. Preheat your oven to 200 ° C. In an increased baking dish, place slices of goat cheese and bake for 8 minutes.
2. Over medium to high heat, place a dry frying pan and toast pumpkin leaves until its color pops, this can be done while baking goat cheese.
3. Reduce heat, add to butter and leave to boil until it gives a soothing nutritional aroma and turns golden brown.

4. Then, pour in Balsamic vinegar and boil for a few minutes. Remove from the heat. Arrange baby spinach on a plate, add in cooked cheese and balsamico butter.

Avocado and Halloumi Cheese Salad

Ingredients:

- 2/3 cucumber
- 2/3 lemon, optional
- ¼ cup sour cream
- salt and pepper to taste.
- 1 avocado
- 8 oz halloumi cheese
- 1 tbsp olive oil
- 1 tbsp butter for frying
- 1 tbsp pistachio nuts

Directions: :

1. Cut the cheese into serving size slices. On medium heat, fry the paneer in butter until it becomes golden. Fry each side for a few minutes. Serve with Sour Cream, Half Avocado, Pistachio Nuts, Cucumber and Vased

Lemon. Season with black pepper and salt and olive oil on the salad.

Feta Cheese and Chicken Salad

Ingredients:

- 1 tomato
- ¼ cup olive oil
- Black pepper and salt to taste
- 6 ounces feta cheese
- 8 black olives
- ½ pound rotisserie chicken
- 1 ounce lettuce

Directions: :

2. Cut the tomatoes and place them on a large plate with lettuce, black olives, chicken and feta cheese. Season with black pepper and salt and serve with olive oil.

Coal slaw

Ingredients:

- ½ teaspoon salt
- 1 pinch black pepper
- A pinch of fennel seeds, optional
- ¼ Vased Lemon, Juice
- ½ tbsp Dijon mustard
- ¼ pound green cabbage
- ¼ cup mayonnaise

Directions: :

3. Take out the core and chop the cabbage with the use of a mandol, cheese slicer or food processor.
4. In a medium-sized bowl, place chopped cabbage, add lemon juice and add salt.
5. Mix together and allow the cabbage to sit for a little wilt for 8 minutes.

6. Pour out excess liquid. Mix in mustard, mayonnaise and cabbage mixture. Season

Orange and Cranberry Muffins

Ingredients:

- Coconut flour, ¼ cups
- 3 large eggs
- Orange zest, 1 tablespoon
- Baking soda, ¼ teaspoon
- Dried cranberries, unsweetened, ½ cup
- Sea salt, ½ teaspoon
- Olive oil or coconut oil, ¼ cup (extra virgin olive oil or coconut oil is recommended)
- Monk fruit or stevia, ¼ cup

Directions: :

1. This is an easy recipe to assemble and bake within a short period. To begin, line and lightly grease a muffin tray with either paper or silicone cups.

2. Add the baking soda, sea salt, and coconut flour together to be blended well using a food processor.
3. Preheat the oven to a temperature of 350 degrees. In the food processor, add in the eggs, sweetener, and orange zest and continue to pulse the ingredients together until well mixed.
4. Remove the mixture and transfer into a large bowl, then fold in the dried cranberries with a fork or by hand.
5. Using a spoon, scoop the muffin batter into each of the muffin cups, filling cups ½ to a max of 2/3, once cups are filled place in the oven for approximately 18-20 min. Remove the tray to cool slightly, for 5-6 minutes, then gently remove the muffins place on a wire rack to cool.

6. It's safe to keep muffins (sealed) at room temp for three days or the refrigerator for up to one week.

Walnut Bread

Ingredients:

- Walnut butter, ¾ cups
- Chia seeds, 1 tablespoon (You can substitute flax seeds if desired)
- Sea salt, ½ teaspoon
- Caraway seeds or a similar seed or herb, 1 tablespoon
- Monk fruit or stevia, or a similar low carb sweetener, 1 tablespoon
- Almond flour, 1/3 cups
- 4 eggs, lightly whisked or beaten
- Baking powder, 1 teaspoon

Directions: :

1. To prepare for the bread, preheat the oven to a temperature of 350 degrees. Add parchment paper or a silicone mat, and a light sprinkling of butter or grease to a loaf pan (9 x 5 inches). If a silicone tray or pan is used, no mat or parchment paper is needed.
2. Walnut butter can be made from scratch if it is not available in a local store or supermarket.
3. To create walnut butter, add one cup of walnuts to two cups of water, and allow them to sit for about one hour to soften, then drain and pour into a food processor or blender.
4. Pulse the walnuts until they are smooth. In some cases, you may not need to soak the walnuts to create a creamy texture, which is the desired result. The blending process shouldn't take more than 5 minutes in total.

5. Transfer the walnut batter to a large mixing bowl and add in the rest of the ingredients, then place mixture in a loaf pan and in the oven for45-50 minutes or until well done. The center of the loaf should be clean when using a toothpick to test. Let the loaf cool completely. A flat surface is also a good option for cooling the loaf before slicing to serve. Walnut bread keeps well at room temperature in a sealed container or wrapped in plastic for up to 3 days. It can also be refrigerated for up to one week or longer.

Cauliflower Breakfast Bake

Ingredients:

- Spinach, chopped finely, 1 cup
- Olive or avocado oil
- Crispy pieces of bacon or prosciutto (vegan or tempeh bacon bits can also be used)
- 1 cup of grated cheese (parmesan is recommended)
- Cauliflower rice, 5 cups
- 4 large eggs

Directions: :

1. Cauliflower rice can be made from scratch, by shredding one or two heads of cauliflower by hand in a grater or slicing into small florets and pulsing in a food processor.

2. If you need to save time, riced cauliflower is often found in grocery stores, either fresh or frozen. If using frozen, make sure the defrost or thaw before using for best results. To prepare the oven, preheat to a temperature of 375 degrees.
3. Combine the riced cauliflower with ½ of the parmesan cheese, eggs, and spinach in a large bowl. Prepare a large muffin tray with a light greasing of olive or avocado oil, with silicone or paper cups.

4. Scoop the cauliflower and egg mixture into each of the muffin cups, preferably with an ice cream scoop, to fill each portion with 1/3 for each cup.
5. In the center of each muffin, create a small opening or well and sprinkle a small amount of the remaining ½ cup of parmesan cheese and bacon or prosciutto pieces. Bake in the

oven for about 15 minutes and serve immediately, or chill in the refrigerator for later use.

6. These breakfast cups will keep for up to 5 days in the refrigerator and can be easily reheated in the microwave for 30 seconds.

7. Note: if cauliflower is unavailable, broccoli can be used in its place, as it has the same texture and consistency. Broccoli tastes excellent with eggs and cheese and is a natural choice for an alternative. For a vegan option, there are vegetable-based versions of non-dairy cheese and tempeh bacon that can replace their dairy and meat counterparts.

Green Smoothie

Ingredients:

For every cup of water:

- 3 to 6 drops of stevia

- 1/2 cup of ice

- 4 tablespoons of lemon juice

- 1 cup of romaine lettuce

- ½ cup of baby spinach

- ½ mint branch with its stem

- ½ avocado

Directions: :

1. Put all the ingredients in a blender and put it on high speed until it's all smooth.
2. Add more ice if it's too liquid or more water if it's too thick.

Avocado Salad and Cilantro-Pesto Chicken

Ingredients:

Chicken

- 1/4 teaspoon of iodized sea salt
- 1 tablespoon avocado oil
- 4 ounces of skinless, boneless chicken breast, cut into equal strips
- 1 tablespoon of lemon juice

Pesto

- 1/4 teaspoon iodized sea salt
- 2 cups of chopped cilantro
- 1/4 cup of extra-virgin olive oil
- 2 tablespoons of lemon juice
- 1/2 diced avocado
- 2 tablespoons extra-virgin olive oil

- 2 tablespoons of lemon juice
  Sea salt to taste
- 1 1/2 cups chopped romaine lettuce

Directions:
1. Heat the avocado oil in a small pan on high heat.
2. Place the chicken strips in the pan and pour the lemon juice and salt.
3. Fry the chicken strips for 2 minutes; turn them and fry for another 2 minutes, until they're completely cooked.
4. Remove and save.
5. For the Pesto, all you need to do is put the ingredients in a mixer and blend them until they are all smooth.
6. For the dressing, put 1 tablespoon of lemon juice over the avocado, and the bind the other lemon juice tablespoon with the olive oil and salt in a jar and shake until is homogeneous.

Arugula Chicken Salad with Lemon Vinaigrette

Ingredients:

CHICKEN

- 4 ounces of skinless, boneless chicken breast, cut into equal strips
- 1 tablespoon of lemon juice
- Zest of 1/2 lemon (optional)
- 1/4 teaspoon of iodized sea salt
- 1 tablespoon avocado oil

DRESSING

- 1/2 diced avocado
- 2 tablespoons extra-virgin olive oil
- 2 tablespoons of lemon juice
- Sea salt to taste

SALAD

- 1 1/2 cups chopped arugula

- Pan fried mushrooms

Directions: :

1. Heat the avocado oil in a small pan on high heat.
2. Place the chicken strips in the pan and pour the lemon juice and salt. Fry the chicken strips for 2 minutes; turn them and fry for another 2 minutes, until they're completely cooked.
3. Remove and save.
4. For the dressing, put 1 tablespoon of lemon juice over the avocado, and the bind the other lemon juice tablespoon with the olive oil and salt in a jar and shake until is homogeneous.
5. Add to the arugula and mushrooms.
6. Top with the chicken and pour some lemon zest.

Chicken Nori Wrap with Cilantro Dip

Ingredients:

CHICKEN NORI WRAP

- 1 tablespoon of lemon juice
- 1 cup of arugula
- 1 sheet of nori
- 4 green olives in halves
- 1/4 teaspoon of iodized sea salt
- 1 tablespoon avocado oil
- 4 ounces of skinless, boneless chicken breast, cut into equal strips

CILANTRO DIP

- 2 cups of diced cilantro
- 2 tablespoons of lemon juice
- 1/4 cup extra-virgin olive oil
- Iodized sea salt to taste

Directions: :

1. Heat the avocado oil in a small pan on high heat.
2. Place the chicken strips in the pan and pour 1 tablespoon lemon juice and salt.
3. Fry the chicken strips for 2 minutes; turn them and fry for another 2 minutes, until they're completely cooked.
4. Remove and save.
5. Pour the avocado into the other lemon juice tablespoon and add salt.
6. For the dip, just add all the ingredients into a blender and process them.
7. To serve, put the arugula in the bottom half of the nori sheet.
8. Top it with the chicken, lemon-avocado and optionally, olives.
9. Add a little salt if you like.
10. Roll it helping yourself with the bamboo mat if you like and seal the end with a drop of water.

11. Cut it in halves to serve it with the dip.

Guacamole Lettuce Boats

Ingredients:

- 1/2 avocado
- A pinch of iodized sea salt
- 1 tablespoon of chopped onion
- 1 teaspoon of chopped cilantro
- 1 tablespoon of lemon juice
- 4 romaine lettuce leaves, washed and dried

Directions: :

1. To make the guacamole just place all the ingredients in the blender and process them until it's smooth.
2. Then just add the guacamole over the lettuce.

Roasted Broccoli with Cauliflower "Rice" and Pan-Fried Onions

Ingredients:

For the Cauliflower "Rice"

Half a medium head of a riced cauliflower

- 1 tablespoon of avocado oil
- 1 tablespoon of lemon juice
- A pinch of sea salt
- 1/4 teaspoon of curry

For the Broccoli

- 1 1/2 cups of cut broccoli buds
- 1 tablespoon of avocado oil
- A pinch of sea salt

For the Sautéed onions

- 1/2 tablespoon avocado oil
- A pinch of salt
- Diced onions

Directions: :

1. Preheat the oven to 325°F.
2. Sauté the cauliflower in a medium pan with 1 tablespoon of avocado oil, and the lemon juice, curry powder, and a pinch of salt until it is tender, about 3 to 5 minutes.
3. Pass it to a plate and keep it warm. Wipe the pan clean.
4. Put the broccoli in an oven safe plate with 1 tablespoon of the oil.
5. Roast it for 15 minutes, blending it twice, until it is tender.
6. Add a tad of salt.
7. Reheat the frying pan and when it is hot, add the remaining tablespoon avocado oil, the diced onion and a pinch of salt.

8. Fry until tender, stirring often, for about 5 minutes.
9. To serve, place the cauliflower "rice" on a plate and on top of it, the broccoli and stir-fried onions.

Italian Healthy Breakfast

Ingredients:

- 1 tablespoon fresh parsley, chopped
- 4 organic eggs
- Salt and pepper to taste
- ¼ teaspoon red pepper flakes, crushed
- 10 cups fresh baby spinach, chopped
- 1/3 cup scallion, chopped
- 2 tablespoons olive oil

Directions: :

1. Preheat your oven to 400°Fahrenheit.
2. Heat over medium-heat in a pan and cook the scallion for about 5 minutes.
3. Add the red pepper flakes, spinach, and black pepper, and stir for about 5 minutes.
4. Move the spinach mixture, removing excess liquid.

5. Make 4 wells in the spinach mixture.
6. Carefully, break an egg in each well.
7. Bake in oven for 15 minutes or until the egg whites are set.
8. Top with parsley and serve.

Tasty Breakfast Hash

Ingredients:

- 1 tablespoon oregano, fresh chopped
- 1 tablespoon thyme, fresh chopped
- 2 tablespoons fresh lime juice
- 1 cup scallion, chopped
- 1 cup homemade chicken broth
- 4 garlic cloves, minced
- 1 medium white onion, chopped
- 2 celery sticks, chopped
- Salt and black pepper to taste
- 1 ½ lbs. grass-fed boneless chicken breasts, cubed
- 2 tablespoons olive oil, divided
- 2 large sweet potatoes, cubed, peeled

Directions: :

1. Add 1 tablespoon of oil into pan over medium heat and cook the chicken sprinkle with salt and pepper for about 5-minutes.
2. Transfer the chicken to a bowl.
3. With the same pan heat remaining oil over medium heat and sauté celery and onion for about 4 minutes.
4. Add in the garlic and herbs and sauté for about 1 minute.
5. Add the sweet potato and cook for 10 minutes.
6. Add the chicken broth and cook for an additional 10 minutes.
7. Add in the cooked chicken and scallion and cook for 5 minutes.
8. Stir in the lime juice, salt and serve.

Breakfast Food Scramble

Ingredients:

- 2 cups kale, fresh, trimmed and chopped
- 2 tablespoons olive oil
- 4 fresh organic eggs
- Black pepper and salt to taste
- 1 teaspoon garlic powder

Directions: :

1. In a mixing bowl, add eggs and beat well. Set aside.
2. In a skillet, heat the oil over medium heat and cook the kale for 2 minutes.
3. Add eggs and remaining ingredients and cook for 4 minutes stirring often.
4. Serve hot and enjoy!

Butternut Squash Soup

Ingredients:

- 1 butternut squash, roasted, seeded, and flesh removed
- 4 cups of vegetable broth
- ½ cup of chopped onion
- 2 teaspoons of thyme
- 1 cup of coconut milk
- 1 teaspoon of black pepper

Directions: :
1. Bring the four cups of vegetable broth to a boil, then add in the onion, baked squash, thyme, black pepper, and coconut milk.
2. Lower the heat and cook on medium, stirring regularly for another 15-20 minutes.
3. Remove from the stove to cool, and process until smooth in the blender in batches. Pour

the soup again in the same pot so that it can be reheated, then add more thyme, black pepper, and serve.

4. This recipe makes approximately 4-6 servings and can take 1.5 hours to prepare (including roasting the squash).

Ginger Carrot Soup

Ingredients:

- 2 diced onions
- Dried or fresh parsley, for garnish
- 1 cup of coconut milk
- ½ cup of vegan sour cream
- 5 cups of vegetable broth
- 3-4 cups of carrots, sliced
- 2 teaspoons of ground ginger (fresh)
- 1 teaspoon of black pepper

Directions: :

1. Cook the onions, carrots, and olive oil in a cooking pot that is large in size for about eight minutes in medium-heat setting, or until soft.

Green Pea Soup

Ingredients:

- 1 teaspoon of dill (fresh or dried)
- 1 teaspoon of tarragon
- 1 teaspoon of black pepper
- 1 bag of frozen peas
- 2 tablespoons of olive oil
- 1 onion, chopped
- 3 cups of vegetable broth

Directions: :

2. Use a large-sized pot to warm the olive oil in a stove temperature set in medium-heat.
3. Add the onion, simmering for a couple of minutes. Pour the broth and spices (tarragon, dill, and black pepper) and continue to cook, then increase the heat so that it begins to boil.

4. Lower the heat and add in the peas and cook on low-medium for about 10-15 minutes until peas are tender, then remove and chill. Use a food processor to pulse the soup batch by batch. Serve hot or cold.
5. This recipe makes 4-6 servings and takes about 30 minutes.

Super nutrient Smoothie

Ingredients:

- 1 cup unsweetened almond milk
- ½ cup raspberries
- ½ a thumb size piece of fresh ginger skin removed and grated or minced
- 1 spoonful of almond butter
- 1 handful of chopped kale with stalk removed
- ½ cup blueberries

Directions: :

1. Prepare and wash ingredients as necessary.
2. Add all ingredients to a blender and blend until smooth.
3. Pour into glasses and drink immediately.

Fruit, Nut and Seed Oatmeal

Ingredients:

- ½ cup steel cut or other oatmeal
- ½ cup almond milk
- ¼ cup granola
- ½ cup mixed berries (Blueberries, raspberries, strawberries or acai)
- ¼ cup mixed nuts (Brazil, Hazelnuts, Pecan, Almonds, Walnuts, cashew, etc.)
- 2 tablespoons mixed seeds (pumpkin, chia, flax, sunflower, sesame, hemp, etc.)

Directions: :
1. To eat cold, add all ingredients to a bowl and mix to combine.
2. To eat hot add the oatmeal and almond milk to a saucepan.
3. Heat through gently for a few minutes until it begins to thicken.
4. Remove from heat and place mix into a bowl, add the remaining ingredients and mix to combine – eat immediately.

Green Power Smoothie

Ingredients:

- 1 handful of spinach or kale
- 1 ripe banana
- 1 cup of your favorite plant -based milk (almond, soy, or coconut)
- 1 tablespoon of nut butter (almond, peanut, or cashew) 1 scoop of plant -based protein powder or 1 tablespoon of chia seeds (optional)
- Ice cubes (optional)

Directions: :

1. Place the spinach or kale, ripe banana, plant-based milk, nut butter, and optional protein powder or chia seeds into a blender.
2. Blend on high until smooth and creamy.

3. If desired, add ice cubes and blend again until chilled.
4. Pour into a glass and enjoy this vibrant green smoothie packed with fiber, vitamins, and minerals to fuel your day.

Citrus Sunrise Juice:

Ingredients:

- 2 oranges

- 1 grapefruit

- 1 lemon

- 1 teaspoon of grated ginger (optional)

Directions: :

1. Cut the oranges, grapefruit, and lemon in half and squeez e out the juice using a citrus juicer or your hands.
2. Strain the juice to remove any pulp or seeds.
3. If desired, grate fresh ginger and add it to the juice for a
4. zingy kick.
5. Stir well and pour into a glass.
6. Savor this citrus -packed juice, high in vitamin C a nd antioxidants, for a refreshing and invigorating start to your day.

Berry Blast Smoothie

Ingredients:

- 1 cup of mixed berries (strawberries, blueberries, raspberries)
- 1 ripe banana
- 1 cup of plant -based milk or yogurt (almond, soy, or coconut)
- 1 tablespoon of flaxseeds or hemp hearts Ice cubes (optional)

Directions: :

1. Place the mixed berries, ripe banana, plant
2. -based milk or
3. yogurt, and flaxseeds or hemp hearts into a blender.
4. Blend on high until smooth and well combined.
5. If desired, add ice cubes and blend again until chilled.

6. Pour into a glass and enjoy this delicious and antioxidant -
7. rich smoothie, providing a burst of energy and essential nutrients.

Tropical Paradise Smoothie

Ingredients:

- 1 cup of pineapple chunks
- 1 ripe banana
- ½ cup of mango chunks
- 1 cup of coconut water or plant-based milk (coconut or almond)
- Juice of 1 lime

Directions: :

1. Combine the pineapple chunks, ripe banana, mango chunks, coconut water or plant-based milk, lime juice, and mint leaves (if using) in a blender.
2. Blend until smooth and creamy.
3. Pour into a glass and imagine yourself in a tropical paradise as you enjoy this refreshing and revitalizing smoothie.

Pancake with Coconut Mochi

Ingredients:

- One cup of mochiko, or sticky rice flour
- 1-/4 cup of sugar
- One teaspoon of powdered sugar
- One cup of coconut cream
- Half a cup of coconut shreds
- Two egg
- Two teaspoons of coconut oil, melted
- A dash of salt
- Extra coconut shreds for the garnish

Directions:

1. Mix the glutinous rice flour, sugar, baking powder, and a small amount of salt in a bowl.
2. Mix the eggs, shredded coconut, melted coconut oil, and coconut milk in a separate bowl.

3. Stir the dry ingredients into the wet mixture gradually until they are just mixed. To enable the mochi to absorb the flavours, let the batter sit for ten minutes.
4. A nonstick pan should be heated to medium heat. Spoon about 1/4 cup of batter into the pan, smoothing it out a little. Cook until surface bubbles appear, then turn and continue cooking until golden on the other side.
5. These Coconut Mochi Pancakes will bring a flavour of the tropics to your breakfast table. Top with more shredded coconut and serve warm.

Eggplant Casserole for a Large Gathering

Ingredients:

- To taste, add salt and pepper.
- Six cups of cubed bread
- Two cups of cheddar cheese, shredded
- Fresh herbs to decorate
- One pound sausage for breakfast
- One sliced onion
- One sliced bell pepper
- Eight big eggs
- Two cups of milk
- One teaspoon of mustard dijon

Directions:

1. Cook the morning sausage until browned in a pan. Cook the bell pepper and chopped onion until they are tender. Put away.

2. Mix the eggs, milk, Dijon mustard, pepper, and salt in a bowl.
3. Place half of the bread cubes, half of the sausage mixture and half of the shredded cheddar cheese in a baking dish that has been oiled. Turn the layers over.
4. Make sure the whisked egg mixture gets into all the crevices and nooks of the layers by evenly pouring it over them.
5. Let the bread absorb the liquid by leaving the dish alone for fifteen minutes. Bake for 45 minutes, or until the top is brown and the eggs are set, at 350°F (175°C) in a preheated oven.
6. Serve this Breakfast Casserole for a Crowd with fresh herb garnish, cut into squares, and watch as every brunch lover grins.

Green Bread with Bananas

Ingredients:

- 3 plump bananas
- One cup of raw spinach
- Two cups flour (all-purpose)
- One tsp baking soda
- Half a teaspoon of salt
- Add chocolate chips or chopped nuts for an added treat.
- Half a cup of yoghurt
- 1-/4 cup of honey
- 1/4 cup melted coconut oil
- Two egg
- One tsp vanilla essence

Directions:

1. Set the oven temperature to 350°F (175°C). Lightly oil and dust a regular loaf pan.
2. Put eggs, melted coconut oil, Greek yoghurt, ripe bananas, fresh spinach, and vanilla essence in a blender. Mix until homogeneous.
3. Blend the Dry Ingredients. Mix the baking soda, salt, and flour in a separate basin.
4. After adding the wet ingredients to the dry, mix just until incorporated. Add chocolate chips or chopped nuts, if preferred, to give it even more flavour.
5. Pour the mixture into the loaf pan that has been prepared, and bake for about 50 minutes, or until a toothpick inserted into the loaf pan comes out clean. When the top of the green banana bread becomes aromatic and golden, it is done.

6. After letting the green banana bread sit in the pan for ten or so minutes, move it to a wire

rack to finish cooling. After cool, cut into appetising chunks.
7. Savour the deliciousness of this Green Banana Bread, where the richness of ripe bananas is complemented with a faint flavour of spinach. It's a delicious way to eat your veggies without realising it, making breakfast or snack time healthier.

Two Ways of French Toast

Ingredients:

- Half a cup of milk
- One tsp vanilla essence
- A little cinnamon pinch
- Using butter to cook
- Traditional French Toast
- Four thick bread slices (such as challah or brioche)
- Two big eggs

Frappeted French Bread

- One tsp vanilla essence
- Using butter to cook
- Dusting powdered sugar
- Four large pieces of bread
- Four ounces of softened cream cheese

- 1/4 cup of your preferred fruit preserves
- Two big eggs
- Half a cup of milk

Directions:

1. Whisk together eggs, milk, cinnamon, and vanilla essence in a small bowl. Make sure to cover both sides of each slice of bread after dipping it into the mixture.
2. Add a pat of butter to a pan or griddle that has been heated to medium heat. Cook until both sides of each piece of bread are golden brown.
3. Spread two pieces of bread with softened cream cheese for the filled variation. Spread the fruit preserves over the other two pieces. One slice of cream cheese and one slice of preserves should be used to make sandwiches.

4. Beat the eggs, milk, and vanilla extract in another bowl.
5. Make sure every sandwich is well covered by dipping it into the egg mixture. Cook on the skillet until golden brown on both sides.
6. For a traditional take and an added sweetness, sprinkle your French toast, two ways, with powdered sugar.
7. Whether you choose the decadent-filled version or the traditional simplicity, these French toasts are a delicious breakfast option.

Bibimbap

Ingredients:

- 16oz "Rice" (prepared - Cauliflower, Basmati, or Shirataki)
- 16oz [450g] Spinach (parboiled and squeezed of excess water, or frozen and chopped)
- 1 Avocado (sliced into strips)
- ½ pound [230g] Meat, or Vegan Protein (optional)
- 4 Eggs
- 4 Tbsp [60mL]
- 4 Carrots (julienned, matchsticks, or spiralized)
- 8 Shiitake Mushrooms (sliced)
- 1 ½ cups [350g] Cucumber (peeled, seeded, sliced into thin strips)

- 1 medium Zucchini (peeled, seeded, sliced into thin strips, or spiralized)

Gochujang Sauce

- 2 Tbsp [30mL] Toasted Sesame Oil
- 1 Tbsp [15mL] Sesame Seeds
- Iodized Sea Salt to taste

Directions:

1. Prepare your rice.
2. Immerse the cucumber in a bath of sea salt and cold water and let sit 20 minutes or more.
3. Parboil the spinach, then drain thoroughly, squeezing out any excess water by pressing gently on it. Add sesame oil and sesame seeds, and let it sit.
4. Separately, divide the rest of the avocado/olive oil and cook each ingredient in a different pan: the carrots, mushrooms, zucchini, and meat or vegan protein if adding. Add a dash of salt to each.

5. Fry the 4 eggs separately, adding a dash of salt to each. Traditionally, these are cooked sunny side up. This will add a splash of gold to the center of your dish.
6. Layer the cooked ingredients in 4 separate bowls, and divide the portions evenly. Begin with the rice at the base, then arrange the cooked vegetables on top of the rice in a ring around the edge. In the center you can add the meat or vegan protein, and then top with an egg, or egg substitute.
7. Serve with a bowl of gochujang sauce that people may add, according to their taste, as well as kimchi and coconut aminos to put on top.

Braised Short Ribs (galbi jim)

Ingredients:

- 3 lbs [1.5kg] English-Cut Short Ribs (also called "thick cut")
- 2 Sweet Potatoes (cut into cubes)
- 2 Carrots (cut in 2 inch lengths)

Spices and liquids:

- 6 Tbsp [90mL] Coconut Aminos
- 2 Tbsp [30mL] Mirin
- 1 Tbsp [15mL] Toasted Sesame Seeds
- 1 Tbsp [15mL] Sesame Oil
- Iodized Sea Salt to taste
- 4 cloves Garlic (finely chopped)
- 1 Onion (grated)
- 3 Scallions (finely chopped)

- ½ cup [120mL] Avocado Oil
- 5 Tbsp [75mL] Swerve (or 25 drops stevia, or a blend of the two)

Directions:

1. Score the ribs (thinly cut across the meat) so they can absorb more of the braising liquid.
2. In a large pot, add all the spices and liquids together and mix.
3. Add the ribs, and immerse in the liquid, making sure they're thoroughly covered in sauce. When resting, the sauce should come up about ½ the level of the ribs.
4. Cover the pot with a tight-fitting lid, and bring to a boil.
5. Once boiling, spoon more sauce over the top of the meat, and turn the heat down to a low simmer. Cook for at least one hour, but two is best for incredibly soft meat.

6. 40 minutes before the end of the cook time, add in the sweet potatoes and carrots, stirring so they are immersed in the caramelizing liquid.
7. Alternatively, cook everything in a slow cooker for 4 hours, or in an instant pot on high for 30 minutes.
8. Serve, and enjoy!

Bulgogi

Ingredients:

- 16oz [450g] Meat, Roasting Vegetables, or Vegan Protein (thinly sliced)

Marinade:

- 3 Scallions (chopped)
- 3 cloves Garlic (chopped)
- 5 Drops Stevia, or 1 tsp [5mL] Monk Fruit
- 2 tsp [10mL] Rice Vinegar
- 2 Tbsp [30mL] Toasted Sesame Seeds
- 1 Tbsp [15mL] Toasted Sesame Oil
- Iodized Sea Salt and Pepper to taste
- 1 Onion (thin strips)
- ¼ cup [60mL] Oil (Extra Virgin Olive, Coconut, or Avocado)

- 3 Tbsp [45mL] Coconut Aminos
- 2 Tbsp [30mL] Swerve, or Sweetener

Directions:

1. In a bowl, stir all the ingredients together except the meat, or roasting vegetables, until the sauce is thoroughly mixed. Add salt and pepper to taste before you add in raw meat.
2. Add thinly sliced strips of meat, vegan meat, or vegetables to the marinade, or if you're going to save some marinade for later, add some marinade to the meat and store the remaining sauce in the refrigerator, or freezer.
3. Refrigerate the meat and marinade mix for at least 30 minutes, but it's best overnight.
4. In a pan over medium heat, stir-fry the meat and marinade mix until the meat is well-done, and the sauce caramelized – about 10 minutes.

5. Alternatively, in an oven tray add the ingredients and bake on 375F [190C] for 15 minutes. But for best results, grill the chicken on a medium hot grill for 3 minutes on each side.
6. As you're doing this, you can caramelize the marinade that it was in and when it's reduced, pour it over the grilled chicken.
7. Serve over rice, noodles, or tofu, or as a topping in another dish, and enjoy!

Bulgogi Chicken

Ingredients:

- 32oz [900g] prepared Rice or Noodles (to serve - Basmati, Cauliflower, Shirataki, Glass Noodles, Rice Noodles, or Foodles)
- 2 pounds [900g] boneless Chicken Thighs, or Roasting Vegetables
- 1 Red Onion (minced)
- 2 cloves Garlic (minced or crushed)
- 1 inch [2.5cm] Ginger (grated)
- ¼ cup [60g] Scallions (chopped)
- ¼ cup [60g] Toasted Sesame Seeds
- 3 Tbsp [45mL] Coconut Aminos
- 1 Tbsp [15mL]

Gochujang Sauce

- 1 Tbsp [15mL] Swerve, or Sweetener
- 1 Tbsp [15mL] Toasted Sesame Oil
- ¼ cup [60mL] Rice Vinegar
- ¼ tsp [2mL] Iodized Sea Salt

Directions:

1. Slice the chicken thighs, or roasting vegetables into 1-2 inch wide strips going the longest way.
2. In a large bowl, combine all ingredients (save a pinch of green onions as a garnish, if you like) and stir thoroughly so that the chicken strips, or roasting vegetables, are evenly coated. Marinate for 60 minutes, or overnight.

3. Over medium-high heat flame, grill the chicken strips, or roasting vegetables for 2-3 minutes on each side, or if pan frying, about 5 minutes on each side over medium-high heat. For cassava, cook on a lower heat until tender, as raw cassava is toxic with cyanide.
4. Serve over "rice," "noodles," or "tofu" and garnish with the remaining green onions.
5. Refrigerate leftovers for up to 1 week, or 1 month in the freezer.

APPLE PIE SMOOTHIE

Ingredients:

- Components for 4 portions:
- 1 tsp ground cinnamon.
- 4 scoop vanilla, vegan protein powder.
- 1 tsp ground nutmeg.
- 1 tsp stevia (optional) if your protein powder is rather sweetened you will not require this.
- 4 apples.
- 17 oz coconut yogurt.
- 4 cups of almond milk.
- 4 tbsp chia seeds.
- oz rolled oats.

Directions:

1. Portion the dry active ingredients into a bag or container for each early morning. Reserve

your apples so nobody gets to them before you do!
2. When it is breakfast time roughly chop the apple, discard the core. Add it to the blender with the almond milk, coconut yogurt and the prepped container of dry components.
3. Blend until smooth and delightful!

SPICY PEANUT BUTTER TEMPEH & RICE

Ingredients:

- 22 oz tempeh, cut into 1-inch cubes.

- 6.5 oz wild rice, raw.

- Coconut oil spray.

Sauce:

- 4 tbsp peanut butter.
- 4 tbsp soy Sauce (low sodium).
- 4 tbsp coconut sugar.
- 2 tbsp red chili sauce.
- 2 tsp rice vinegar.
- 2 tbsp ginger.
- 3 cloves of garlic (or garlic paste).
- 6 tbsp water.

Cabbage:

- 5 oz purple cabbage, shaved/finely sliced.

- 1 lime, juice only.

- 2 tsp agave/apple bee-free honey.

- 3 tsp sesame oil.

- Garnish:
- Green onion, chopped.

Directions:

1. Mix all of the ingredients for the spicy peanut sauce.
2. Cut the tempeh into 1-inch (2.5 cm) cubes.
3. Add sauce to the tempeh, stir, cover and marinade in the fridge for 2-3 hours or, preferably, overnight. Tempeh is actually good at soaking up the tastes of the marinade.
4. Preheat the oven to 375° F/190° C cook the rice as per packet directions.
5. Location the tempeh on a nonstick flat pan, spray with some coconut oil, bake in the oven for 25-30 minutes. Conserve any leftover marinade for serving.
6. Mix all of the components for the cabbage in a bowl and set aside to let it marinate.
7. Serve it up: To a bowl or meal preparation container, include tempeh, rice and cabbage.

Scoop a little additional of the Tempeh marinade on the top as a sauce. Garnish with green onion.

VEGAN FRY-UP

Ingredients:

For the hash browns:

- 1 big potato, unpeeled.

- 1 1/2 tbsp peanut butter.

- For the mushrooms and tomatoes:

- 14 cherry tomatoes.

- Sunflower oil.

- 2 tsp maple syrup.

- 1 tsp soy sauce..

- 1/4 tsp smoked paprika.

- 1 large Portobello mushroom, sliced.

For the rushed tofu:

- 349 g pack silken tofu.

- 2 tbsp dietary yeast.

- 1/2 tsp turmeric.

- 1 clove garlic, crushed.//
- 4 vegan sausages.
- 1 x 200 g can baked beans.

Directions:

1. Prepare the potato whole in a large pan of water, boil for 10 minutes then permit and drain pipes to cool. Set aside in the fridge until needed.
2. Heat oven to 200° C/180° C fan/gas six. Put the cherry tomatoes onto a baking tray, drizzle with 2 tsp sunflower oil, season and bake for 30 minutes or until the skins have actually blistered and begin to char. Prepare the beans and sausages following the guidelines on the pack, so they are ready to serve at the very same time as the scrambled tofu.
3. On the other hand, mix the maple syrup, soy sauce and 1/4 tsp smoked paprika together in a big bowl, add the sliced up mushroom and

toss to coat in the mix. Leave to stand while you put 2 tsp sunflower oil into a non-stick frypan and bring it as much as a medium-high heat. Fry the mushroom up until simply beginning to turn golden however not charred. Scoop onto a plate and keep warm until serving.

4. Put 1 tbsp. oil into the frying pan and include a spoonful of the potato mix - you should get about four. Fry for 3-4 minutes each side then drain onto kitchen paper.

5. Fall apart the tofu into your frying pan and sprinkle over the staying ingredients and a great pinch of salt and pepper, if the pan looks a little dry add a splash more oil. Fry for 3-4 minutes or until the tofu is broken into pieces, well coated in the flavoring and hot through.

6. Divide everything in between 2 plates and serve with a hot mug of tea made using soy milk.

MISO RAMEN

Ingredients:

- 5 tbsp miso paste.
- 1 tbsp vegetable oil.
- 8 child pak choi.
- 200 g ready-to-eat beansprouts.
- 2 red chilies, finely sliced on an angle.
- 2 spring onions, carefully sliced on an angle.
- 4 tbsp crispy seaweed.
- 2 tbsp black sesame seeds.
- 1 tbsp sesame oil, to finish.
- 2 tbsp soy sauce.
- 2 1/2 cm piece of ginger, grated.
- 12 shiitake mushrooms.
- 225 g smoked tofu, cut into 4 pieces.
- 2 tbsp liquid amino or tamari.
- 250 g soba noodles.

- 16 ears baby corn.

Directions:

1. Put the miso, 1.5 liters water, soy sauce, ginger and shiitake in a large pan. Stir to blend in the miso, then bring to a very gentle simmer. Keep simmering for 5 minutes.
2. Meanwhile, position the smoked tofu in a shallow bowl and pour over the liquid amino. Turn the tofu pieces over to make sure they are soaked well on both sides.
3. Bring a pan of salted water to the boil. Add the soba noodles, bring back to the boil and cook till just tender, about 5 mins.
4. Add the child corn to the miso broth and cook for a further 4 minutes.
5. Heat the oil in a non-stick frying pan over high heat. Gently place the tofu in the frying pan and cook for 2-3 minutes on each side till browned.

6. As soon as the noodles are cooked, drain them in a colander and rinse under cold water, then divide in between 4 serving bowls. Include the pak choi to the miso broth and get rid of from the heat.
7. Divide the pak choi, infant corn and beansprouts in between the bowls - ladle over the miso broth and include the tofu. Garnish with the chillies, spring onions and crispy seaweed. Sprinkle with sesame seeds, drizzle over the sesame oil and serve straight away.

BALI BOWL WITH TEMPEH, PEANUTS AND TOMATO SAMBAL

Ingredients:

- 2-5 red chillies, seeds eliminated.
- 2 kaffir lime leaves, finely sliced.
- 1/2 tsp palm sugar, or soft brown sugar.
- 1/2 tsp salt.
- 3 tomatoes.
- 2 shallots, or small red onions.
- 4 cloves garlic.

For the tempeh:

- 2 cups red cabbage, shredded.
- 1 carrot, shredded or grated.
- 1 cup green beans, (a large handful).
- 1 tbsp lime juice (juice of half a lime).
- 125 g tempeh, sliced up or fallen apart into little pieces.

- 1/4 cup peanuts.
- 1 tbsp. coconut oil.
- For the salad:
- 1 tsp sesame oil.

For the rice:

- 1 cup red rice, or brown.
- A handful of basil leaves, or fresh herbs of your choice.

Directions:
1. Starting with one chili put all active ingredients into a blender and procedure until reasonably smooth. Taste and include more chilies up until the sambal is at your desired level of spiciness. Adjust flavoring to taste, with more salt or sugar.
2. For the rice:
3. Prepare rice according to packet directions.
4. For the salad:
5. While your rice is cooking, prepare your salad.

6. Bring water to a boil in a little pan. Blanch green beans for three minutes, then get rid of a colander/sieve and run under cold water to cool right away.
7. Put shredded red cabbage, carrot and beans into a blending bowl.
8. Put over the lime juice and sesame oil and toss to coat.
9. To serve:
10. Serve Bali bowls with a portion of red rice and salad, leading with the hot tempeh and peanuts, a handful of fresh herbs, and extra tomato sambal on the side.

SCRAMBLED TOFU BREAKFAST BURRITO

Ingredients:

- 1 12-ounce bundle firm or extra-firm tofu.
- 1 tsp oil (or 1 tbsp (15 ml) water).
- 1 tsp dietary yeast.
- 1/4 tsp sea salt.
- 1 pinch cayenne pepper .
- 1/4 cup minced parsley.
- 3 cloves garlic (minced).
- 1 tbsp hummus (store-bought or DIY).
- 1/2 tsp chili powder.
- 1/2 tsp cumin.

Vegetables:

- 5 whole baby potatoes.
- 1 medium red bell pepper.
- 1 tsp oil.
- 1 pinch sea salt.

- 1/2 tsp ground cumin.

- 1/2 tsp chili powder (not ground chili).

- 2 cups chopped kale.

The rest:

- 3-4 large flour or gluten-free tortillas (ensure vegan-friendly - I like TJ's brand).

- 1 medium ripe avocado (chopped or mashed).

- Cilantro.

- Chunky green or red salsa or hot sauce.

Directions:

1. Preheat oven to 400° F (204° C) and line a baking sheet with parchment paper (use more baking sheets if increasing batch size). In the meantime, likewise, wrap tofu in a clean towel and set something heavy on top - such as a cast-iron skillet - to push out excess wetness. Then fall apart with a fork into fine pieces. Set aside.

2. Add potatoes and red pepper to the baking sheet, drizzle with oil (or water) and spices, and toss to combine. Bake for 15-22 minutes or until fork-tender and a little browned. Include kale in the last 5 minutes of baking to wilt, tossing with the other veggies to integrate seasonings.
3. In the meantime, heat a large skillet over medium heat. As soon as hot, include oil (or water), garlic, and tofu and sauté for 7-10 minutes, stirring often, to slightly brown.
4. In the meantime, to a small blending bowl, include the hummus, chili powder, cumin, nutritional yeast, salt, and cayenne (optional). Continue adding water until the formation of a pourable sauce. Add the spice mix to the tofu and continue cooking over medium heat up until slightly browned - 3-5 minutes.
5. Include generous portions of the roasted vegetables, scrambled tofu, avocado, cilantro,

and a bit of salsa. Continue until all garnishes are used up - about 3-4 large burritos.

6. Delight in instantly for most excellent outcomes. Alternatively, you can package and refrigerate these up to 4 days (or the freezer for 1 month). If heating in microwave, simply microwave or heat in the oven before eating (be sure to eliminate foil).

Avocado and Smoked Salmon Wrap:

Ingredients:

- Nori sheets
- Sliced avocado
- Smoked salmon
- Shredded cucumber
- Sesame seeds

Directions:

1. Lay out a nori sheet and add sliced avocado, smoked salmon, shredded cucumber, and a sprinkle of sesame seeds.
2. Roll it up into a wrap for a savory and satisfying breakfast.

Sweet Potato and Spinach Frittata:

Ingredients:

- Sweet potatoes, grated
- Spinach, chopped
- Pasture-raised eggs
- Garlic powder, salt, and pepper

Directions:

1. Sauté grated sweet potatoes until softened.
2. Add chopped spinach and cook until wilted.
3. Whisk eggs with garlic powder, salt, and pepper, then pour over the vegetables.
4. Bake until the frittata is set for a hearty breakfast.

Coconut Flour Pancakes with Berries

Ingredients:

- Coconut flour
- Almond milk
- Eggs
- Mixed berries for topping

Directions:

1. Mix coconut flour, almond milk, and eggs to make a batter.
2. Cook pancakes and top with fresh mixed berries for a delightful breakfast treat.

Grilled Chicken Salad with Avocado Dressing

Ingredients:

- Grilled chicken breast, sliced
- Mixed greens
- Cherry tomatoes, halved
- Avocado, mashed for dressing
- Olive oil, lemon juice, salt, and pepper

Directions:

1. Arrange mixed greens on a plate, top with grilled chicken and cherry tomatoes.
2. Whisk mashed avocado with olive oil, lemon juice, salt, and pepper for a creamy dressing.

Cauliflower Rice Stir-Fry with Shrimp

Ingredients:

- Cauliflower rice
- Shrimp, peeled and deveined
- Mixed vegetables (bell peppers, broccoli, snap peas)
- Coconut aminos for seasoning

Instructions

1. Stir-fry cauliflower rice and mixed vegetables until tender.
2. Add shrimp and coconut aminos for a flavorful and low-carb stir-fry.

Hot Kale Salad

Ingredients:

- 1 tbsp olive oil
- Heavy Cup Heavy Whipping Cream
- 1 clove of garlic, minced
- 2 ounces feta cheese
- 6 ounces of banana
- 2 ounces butter
- 1 tbsp mayonnaise
- ½ tbsp Dijon mustard
- 1 ounce butter
- Salt and pepper.

Directions:

1. Stir in mayonnaise, heavy cream, olive oil, mustard, and garlic in a small bowl and season with salt and pepper.
2. Wash the buds and slices in bite size portions and remove the hard stem.

3. Over medium heat, place a large frying pan and butter to melt. Fry the pan till it gives a nice color. Season with salt and pepper.
4. Then pour it into a bowl and drip the dressing over the top. Mix well together and serve with crumbled cheese.

Caesar salad

Ingredients:

- 8 oz Chicken Breast
- ½ teaspoon olive oil
- ¼ Romance Lettuce
- 4 ounces bacon
- 2 ounces fresh grated cottage cheese
- Black pepper and salt to taste.

Directions:

1. Combine the dressing ingredients in a medium-sized bowl and whisk. Refrigerate for a while. Preheat your oven to 200 ° C. Then arrange the chicken breasts in an enlarged baking pan. Season the chicken with black pepper and salt to taste, dripping some olive oil on top of the chicken breasts.
2. Bake in the oven for about 10-15 minutes until tender and cooked through. If you wish,

you can also cook the chicken on top of your stove.
3. Then in a frying pan, add a little oil and fry your bacon until it is tender and crisp.
4. Shape the lettuce and arrange as a base on a plate, then add chopped baked chicken and crispy bacon on top.
5. Drizzle with your dressing and sprinkle with a generous amount of grated paneer cheese.

Greek Keto Salad

Ingredients:

- 2 ripe tomatoes
- 1 teaspoon dried parsley
- 2 tablespoons olive oil
- 5 ounces feta cheese
- 8 Black Greek Olives.
- Ion Red Onion
- ¼ teaspoon red wine vinegar
- Umber Cucumber
- 4 green bell peppers

Directions:

1. Cut tomatoes and cucumber into bite size portions. Finely chop red onion and bell peppers. Place on a serving salad plate. Add olives and feta cheese.
2. Drizzle red wine vinegar and olive oil over the salad. Add salt and pepper to taste.

3. Sprinkle with oregano (icing) and enjoy.

Anchovies and yellow-beet salad

Ingredients:

Fresh chives

- 1 baby gemstone lettuce

- 6 oz ripe yellow beets

- Ion Red Onion

- 1 ounce anchovy

- ½ cup mayonnaise

Directions:

1. Cut the ripe yellow beets into dice as well as red onions and anchovies.
2. Mix in a bowl and add mayonnaise.
3. Garnish with finely chopped chives and serve with baby gemstone lettuce.

Niquise

Ingredients:

- 1 egg
- 1 ounce Cherry Tomato
- 5 ounce romaine lettuce
- Ion Red Onion
- salt and pepper to taste
- 5 ounces of fresh green beans
- 2 ounces celery root
- 1 garlic clove, finely chopped

Decoration:

- ¼ Tbsp Dijon mustard
- ½ ounce anchovies
- ¼ cup mayonnaise
- 1 tbsp small capers
- ¼ cup olive oil
- ½ teaspoon fresh parsley

- ½ minced garlic cloves.

Directions:

1. Using a mixer, mix all the ingredients for the dressing and mix until creamy and completely combined and set aside.
2. Boil eggs as a favorite and keep in an ice cold bath to speed up peeling. Slice into wedges. Rinse and peel turnip.
3. Cut into half inch pieces. Rinse and trim green beans and parabil in salted water for 5 minutes. When cooked, rinse in cold water. On medium-high heat, place a pan, add in olive oil and sauté.
4. Add finely chopped garlic and season with pepper and salt.
5. Arrange the letter on a platter. Add tomatoes, eggs, minced tuna, olive onions, turnips and beans. Serve dressing on the side.

Chili soup

Ingredients:

- 1 clove of garlic, crushed
- 1 teaspoon onion powder
- 1 tbsp chili powder
- 24 ounces can crush tomatoes
- ½ teaspoon olive oil
- 1 teaspoon sea salt
- ½ pound ground beef
- , Medium onion, roughly chopped
- C spoon ground canned pepper
- Water cup water
- ½ cup dairy cherry tomatoes
- Oon Spoon Garlic Powder
- Powder Tbsp Cumin Powder

Directions:

1. Fry onion, garlic and ground beef in a pan over medium heat.
2. Then, add fresh tomatoes, can tomatoes, and other spices. Leave to boil over medium to low heat for 15-20 minutes.

Peach Pancakes

Ingredients:

- Cassava flour, 1/4cup
- Seasalt, 1 teaspoon
- Baking soda, ¼ teaspoon
- Baking powder, 1/2 teaspoon
- 2 peaches, ripe. Peeled and sliced into thin slices
- Cinnamon sprinkled over the peaches
- Vanilla extract, 1 teaspoon
- 2 large eggs
- Monk fruit or stevia, 1 teaspoon
- Kefir or coconut yogurt, 5 ounces
- Coconut flour, ¼ cup
- Tapioca, 1/4 cup

- Coconut oil, melted, one tablespoon

Directions:

1. Prepare the oven by preheating to a temperature of 350 degrees and prepare a pie tray or pan with butter.
2. Using a lg bowl, add eggs, sweetener, kefir or coconut yogurt, and vanilla extract.
3. When adding these items into the bowl, gradually pour the coconut oil and whisk it continuously, to avoid the oil from sticking or becoming solid.
4. This is especially a concern if the room temperature is a bit cooler than usual. Combine the cassava flour, coconut flour, sea salt, tapioca flour, baking soda, and baking powder, using a med bowl, and blend well, then gently combine with the wet ingredients,

a little at a time, until a smooth batter is formed.

5. Pour the batter into a pie pan and place the peach slices on top of the batter, then sprinkle with cinnamon evenly. Cinnamon can also be sprinkled or coated over the peaches while mixing ingredients. Cook for 30 min, then test with a toothpick to ensure it comes out clean, which means the pie-pancake is ready. Serve with additional peach slices and whipped cream (coconut or dairy), and cinnamon.

Egg and Arugula

Ingredients:

- 3 eggs
- Olive oil, 3 tablespoons, divided
- Balsamic vinegar, 2 tablespoons
- Sea salt, 1/2 teaspoon
- Fresh Arugula, 2 cups (chopped)

Directions:

1. Using med heat and a lg skillet warm olive oil. Using a sm bowl, whisk the balsamic vinegar, and sea salt together until well combined.
2. In a second bowl, whisk the eggs and add any desired spices, such as black pepper, paprika, etc. until blended.

3. Pour the eggs to scramble in the skillet, mixing evenly until they are well cooked.
4. Remove to a medium bowl, then mix the chopped arugula and drizzle the dressing over the dish to serve

Sweet Potato and Onion Patties

Ingredients:

- 1 large or 2 med sweet potatoes
- 1 small onion, white or yellow, diced finely
- 1 large or 2 small or medium eggs
- Sea salt / ground black pepper, as desired
- Paprika, ½ tsp
- Chili-pepper, ½ teaspoon
- Olive oil for cooking

Directions:

1. To prepare the sweet potatoes, scrub, peel and slice them into halves, thirds, or sizes that are comfortable to shred through a grate.

2. Using a large grater, shred all the sweet potato and set aside.
3. Peel the onion and slice in half and shred or finely dice to mix with the sweet potato.
4. Mix these two ingredients well with a fork, then add in the eggs, whisking and blending evenly. Add in the sea salt, black pepper, paprika, and chili pepper, to create the patty batter.
5. Over med heat and a lg skillet warm olive oil. As the skillet is in the process of warming up, form 2-inch or 3-inch sized patties to fry on both sides of the skillet. If desired, add a light sprinkle of sea salt and/or the spices and seasoning of your choice.
6. Cook on each side for about 2 minutes, or until the result is golden in color. Serve

immediately garnished with sliced parsley, coriander, and/or sour cream.

Cabbage-Kale Sauté with Salmon and Avocado

Ingredients:

- 1/2 diced avocado
- 1 1/2 cups of thinly sliced cabbage (green, bok choi or your preferred cabbage)
- 1/2 red onion, thinly sliced
- 3 ounces of wild-caught salmon
- 4 pinches of iodized sea salt
- 3 tablespoons of lemon juice
- 3 tablespoons of avocado oil

Directions: :

1. Mix diced avocado with 1 tablespoon of lemon juice and a drop of salt.
2. Heat a pan to medium heat.
3. Then, add 2 tablespoons of oil and all of the cabbage and onion.
4. Fry for 10 minutes or until it's tender, stirring once in a while, and add two pinches of salt.
5. Remove.

6. Now add the last tablespoon of oil to the skillet, raise the heat and put in the salmon.
7. Add the rest of the lemon juice and a pinch of salt.
8. Sear it 3 minutes each side and you can serve.

Coconut and Almond Flour Muffin

Ingredients:

- 1 tablespoon of melted coconut oil
  1 tablespoon of olive or macadamia nut oil
- 1 pack of stevia
- 1/2 teaspoon of baking powder
- 1 tablespoon of coconut flour
- 1 tablespoon of almond flour
- 1 pinch of iodized sea salt
- 1 tablespoon of water
- 1 large lightly beaten egg

Directions:

1. Place all of the ingredients in a mug that's somewhere between 8 to 12 ounces and mix them well with a spatula scraping the bottom and sides of the mug.
2. Let it stand and microwave it for 1 minute.

3. Let it stand again and microwave them for another 30 seconds.
4. Remove the mug and invert it using a pot holder.
5. Let it stand for a couple of minutes before you eat it.

Cranberry-Orange Muffin

Ingredients:

1. 1 tablespoon of orange zest
2. 1/2 cup of unsweetened cranberries
3. 1/4 cup of coconut flour
4. 1/4 teaspoon of baking soda
5. 1/4 teaspoon of sea salt
6. 1/4 cup of melted coconut oil
7. 1/4 cup of xylitol
8. 3 large eggs

Directions:

1. Preheat the oven to 350°F.
2. Line a 6-cup muffin tin with paper liners.
3. Then, put the flour and baking soda in a food processor.
4. Add the oil, the xylitol, eggs, and zest.
5. Process it until it's blended.

6. Remove the blade and mix in the cranberries with a spatula.
7. Scoop the mix into the tins and bake for 20 minutes.
8. Let them cool for 15 minutes before you eat them.

Cinnamon and Flaxseed Muffin

Ingredients:

- 1 pack of stevia
- 1 tablespoon of coconut oil
- 1/4 cup of grounded flaxseed
- 1 teaspoon cinnamon
- 1 large pastured egg
- 1 teaspoon of baking powder

Directions:

1. Put all of the ingredients in a mug that's somewhere between 8 to 12 ounces and mix them well with a spatula scraping the bottom and sides of the mug.
2. Let them sit for a few seconds, and then microwave on high temperature for 1 minute.
3. Let it stand for a few seconds and check if the muffin is still wet in the center if so, cook for another 15 seconds.

4. Remove the mug and invert it using a pot holder.
5. Let it stand for a couple of minutes before you eat it.

Shakshuka

Ingredients:

- Two tsp olive oil
- One-fourth teaspoon of cayenne pepper, or to taste
- One 28-ounce can of crushed tomatoes
- To taste, add salt and pepper.
- 4–6 big eggs
- To garnish, fresh parsley
- Bread that is crusty to serve
- One sliced onion
- One sliced bell pepper
- 3 minced garlic cloves
- One teaspoon of cumin powder
- One teaspoon of coriander powder
- One-half tsp smoked paprika

Directions:

1. Cooking Aromatics
1. Set a big skillet with olive oil on medium heat. Saute the bell pepper and sliced onion till they get tender.
2. Blend Spices
3. Add the cayenne pepper, smoked paprika, ground cumin, ground coriander, and chopped garlic. Give the spices a minute to toast so that the delicious scent fills your kitchen.
4. Cook the tomato sauce.
5. Add the crushed tomatoes, season with salt and pepper, and cook until the sauce
6. thickens about 15 to 20 minutes.

Orange-Cranberry Morning Bread

Ingredients:

- Two cups flour (all-purpose)

- The orange zest
- One-third cup of just-squeezed orange juice
- One-third cup of olive oil
- One big egg
- One tsp vanilla essence
- One cup of sugar, grated
- One and a half tsp baking powder
- One-half tsp baking soda
- Half a teaspoon of salt
- One cup of freshly split cranberries

Directions:

1. Set the oven temperature to 350°F (175°C). Lightly oil and dust a regular loaf pan.
2. Combine Dry Elements
3. Combine flour, baking soda, baking powder and a pinch of salt in a large bowl.
4. Add Orange Zest and Cranberries.

5. Fold the orange zest and the chopped cranberries gently into the dry ingredients. This gives each bite an explosion of delicious fruit.
5. Mix the moist ingredients.
6. Mix the egg, vanilla extract, vegetable oil, and orange juice in another dish.
6. Mix the batter.
7. After adding the wet ingredients to the dry, mix just until incorporated. A few lumps are perfectly OK; just take care not to overmix.
7. Put in a pan and cook
8. After preheating the loaf pan, pour the batter into it and level the top. When a toothpick put into the centre comes out clean, bake for about 50 minutes.
8. Chill and Cut
9. After letting the Cranberry-Orange Breakfast Bread set in the pan for approximately fifteen minutes, move it to a wire rack to finish cooling. After cooling, cut into enticing pieces.

9. Savour Fruity Delights
10. This Cranberry-Orange Breakfast Bread combines the tartness of cranberries with
11. the zesty flavour of oranges to create a delicious breakfast treat that can be savoured with coffee or on its own.

Vegan Breakfast Burrito

Ingredients:

- 1 wheat or maize tortilla wrap (vegan)
- 1/2 cup refried beans (heated)
- 1 small avocado peeled, de-seeded and sliced
- ¼ cup of sliced romaine lettuce
- 1 diced fresh tomato
- 2 tablespoons of salsa (try making your own)
- ½ lime
- ¼ cup cilantro (chopped)
- Siracha hot sauce

Directions:

1. Use a toaster to warm the tortilla wrap gently.
2. Place the warm wrap on a plate and add the refried beans, avocado, lettuce, tomato and salsa.

3. Add a splash of sriracha hot sauce to taste and close the wrap.
4. Garnish with a squeeze of lime and some chopped cilantro.
5. Serve immediately.

Chickpea and Apple Pesto Pasta

Ingredients:

- 3 cups of cooked whole wheat pasta or non-wheat pasta if preferred (Rigatoni or Fusilli are good choices)
- 2 packed cups of arugula (rocket) or spinach
- 2/3 cup chickpeas ready cooked and rinsed
- 1/3 cup basil pesto
- ¼ cup apple, cored and cubed
- 2 tablespoons of lime juice

Directions:

1. Cook the pasta by following the instructions given by the manufacturer. Drain and rinse thoroughly.
2. Put the apple, chickpeas and lime into a bowl and mix together until combined.

3. Add the pasta and pesto to the bowl and toss it together.
4. Finally, add the greens and gently combine it into the rest of the ingredients.
5. The bowl can be brought to the table for people to help themselves, or you can plate it up into individual bowls.
6. Add freshly ground black pepper and freshly squeezed lime to taste.

Spicy Vegetable Noodle Soup

Ingredients:

- 4 ounces of Udon (or other variety) noodles (cooked according to instructions on the packet).

- 3 cups of vegetable broth (preferably homemade. If shop bought choose low or no sodium varieties).

- 1 teaspoon of chili sauce or sriracha (add more to taste if you like it hot).
- 1 cup (packed) Bok choy, kale or dark leafed cabbage.
- 1/3 cup mushrooms, sliced.
- ¼ cup green onion, sliced.
- 3 cloves of fresh garlic minced or grated.
- ½ thumb size piece of fresh ginger, peeled and grated.
- 1 lime cut into quarters.

Directions:

1. While the noodles are cooking bring the vegetable broth and chili sauce to the boil on the stove and then turn down to simmer.
2. Add the mushrooms, onion and garlic to the broth and after 1 minute add the greens and simmer for a further 2 to 3 minutes until the greens have wilted.

3. Add the cooked noodles to the broth and vegetable mixture and combine through.
4. Serve in bowls and eat immediately while hot.

Mixed Vegetable Sichuan

Ingredients:

- 2 tablespoons sesame oil
- 4 garlic cloves, crushed
- A large thumb size piece of fresh ginger, peeled and grated
- 1 2/3 cups of carrots sliced into very thin strips
- 1 red bell pepper, deseeded and sliced into very thin strips
- 2 cups shiitake mushrooms sliced (you can use other mushrooms if you can't find shiitake).
- 2 cups mange tout (snow peas)
- 3 tablespoons of soy sauce
- 3 tablespoons crunchy peanut butter
- 4 cups beansprouts

- 2 cups rice, cooked washed in cold water and drained

Directions:

1. Heat the sesame oil in a preheated wok or deep skillet and fry the ginger and carrots for 2 minutes.
2. Add the red pepper and garlic and stir-fry for another 2 minutes. Then add the mushrooms and mange tout and stir-fry for a further minute.
3. In a small bowl, combine the soy sauce and peanut butter until mixed thoroughly.
4. Put on a kettle of water to boil.
5. Make a space in the center of the stir-fried vegetables with a wooden spoon so that the base of the wok is visible. Pour in the sauce and bring to the boil, stirring continually until it starts to thicken.

6. Finally, add the beansprouts and toss them through the vegetables to coat thoroughly with the sauce.
7. Pour the kettle of boiling water through the pre-cooked rice and drain.
8. Plate up the rice into individual bowls and place the stir fry on top. Serve immediately.

Australian Breakfast Omelet

Ingredients:

- 2 tablespoons olive oil, divided
- 1 teaspoon chives, fresh minced
- 1 small avocado, peeled, pitted and cubed into small pieces
- Salt and freshly ground black pepper to taste
- 4 large organic eggs
- 2 small beets, peeled and spiralized with Blade C

Directions:

1. Using a large pan, heat 1 tablespoon olive oil over medium heat and cook the beet noodles for about 7 minutes.
2. Remove from heat and set aside.
3. Add to your mixing bowl, salt, pepper and eggs then beat well.

4. Heat the remaining oil in large frying pan over medium heat.
5. Add your egg mixture to your pan and spread the eggs over pan using a wooden spoon.
6. Cook the egg mixture for 12 minutes.
7. Place the beets and avocado over the eggs.
8. Carefully, fold the omelet over the beet noodles and avocado and cook for 2 minutes.
9. Cut the omelet into 3 portions and serve with the chives for garnish.

Avocado Cups

Ingredients:

- 4 organic eggs
- 2 ripe avocados, halved, pitted and scoop out about 2 tablespoons of flesh
- 1 tablespoon chives, fresh minced
- Salt and freshly ground black pepper to taste

Directions:

1. Preheat your oven to 425°Fahrenheit.
2. Arrange the avocado halves in a small baking dish, with the cut side facing upwards.
3. In a mixing bowl, break an egg then transfer it into an avocado half.
4. Repeat this step with the remaining eggs.
5. Carefully, place into your oven and bake for 20 minutes or until you have reached the desired doneness reached.

6. Serve immediately, sprinkle with salt and pepper and chives

Banana Pancakes

Ingredients:

- 1 teaspoon apple cider vinegar
- ½ teaspoon ground cinnamon
- ¼ teaspoon organic baking powder
- ¼ cup coconut flour
- ½ teaspoon organic vanilla extract
- 1 tablespoon organic honey
- 1 ripe banana, peeled and mashed
- 2 organic eggs
- ½ cup unsweetened almond milk
- Pinch of salt
- 2 teaspoons olive oil

Directions:

1. In a large mixing bowl, mix baking powder, flour, cinnamon, and salt.

2. In another bowl, add egg, banana, almond milk, honey, vinegar, and vanilla, beat well until well combined.
3. Add the mixture into your flour mixture and mix well.
4. Grease a frying pan with olive oil and heat over medium heat.
5. Add the desired amount of mixture and cook for 3 minutes.
6. With a spatula, flip over the pancake and cook for 2 more minutes.
7. Repeat with remaining mixture and serve warm.

www.ingramcontent.com/pod-product-compliance
Lightning Source LLC
LaVergne TN
LVHW010224070526
838199LV00062B/4717